Roger Hurn used to be an actor in 'The Exploding Trouser Company'. He has also appeared on 'The Weakest Link' on TV – and he won!

Now he spends his time writing and telling stories. His scariest and spookiest experience came when he went to an old ghost town in the Wild West of the USA. This gave him the idea for **Spook Squad**.

He hopes you enjoy reading the Spook Squad's adventures as much as he enjoyed writing them.

Spook Squad
The Scream Team
by Roger Hurn
Illustrated by Peter Richardson

Published by Ransom Publishing Ltd.
Radley House, 8 St. Cross Road, Winchester, Hampshire
SO23 9HX, UK
www.ransom.co.uk

ISBN   978 184167 076 8
First published in 2012

The Scream Team

by Roger Hurn

Ransom

Dead End Junction

The Ghost Train Railway

Vlad the Bad's Castle

Ghouls' Graveyard

The Isle of Fright

It's the dead centre of Otherworld!

The Wraith Pits
They really are the pits!

The Haunted Pyramid
Your mummy warned you about this place

Here There Be Dragons

Banshee Bay
Where the wind never stops howling!

They sleep in the day and fight knights!

Otherworld

GOBLIN GULCH
The home of
messy eaters

FANG MOUNTAINS
You'll say 'Fangs for
nothing' if you try to
climb them

KRAKEN LAKE

Swim at
your
own risk!

SPOOK CITY

THE ZOMBI RIVER

WEREWOLF WOODS
Avoid when the
moon is full!

Otherworld

Where is Otherworld?

The far side of a shadow.

Who lives there?

Ghouls, ghosts, long-leggedy beasties and things that go bump in the night.

Why do the creatures who live there come to our world?

To make mischief.

Rhee the Banshee answers readers' questions.

How do they get here?

> They slip through secret gateways when you're not looking.

Can humans go to Otherworld?

> Yes, but they shouldn't.

Why not?

> Because they never come back.

Why not?

> Trust me – you really **DO NOT** want to know!

Meet The SPOOK SQUAD

Emma

FYI: She spends her life getting hold of the wrong end of the stick.

Loves: Getting the point.

Hates: Muddy sticks.

Fact: She doesn't like vampires – she thinks they're a pain in the neck.

Roxy

FYI: Don't call her 'Ginger' - unless you want to eat your dinner through a straw.

Loves: Being a strawberry blonde.

Hates: Seeing red.

Fact: She reckons cannibal goblins are messy eaters, so she won't be joining their fang club.

Nita

FYI: This girl gets gadgets. Give her a paper clip, a rubber band, a tin can and an A4 battery and she'll rig up a gizmo that'll blow your gran's pop socks off.

Loves: Fixing things.

Hates: Fixing it – if it ain't broke.

Fact: Nita has invented ghost-proof wheels for her bike. They don't have any spooks!

Leena

FYI: If she was any sharper you could use her to slice bread.

Loves: Big words.

Hates: Small minds.

Fact: She prefers whatwolves and whenwolves to werewolves.

Aunt Rhee

FYI: Rhee's not the kind of aunt who gives you a woolly jumper for Christmas.

Loves: Walking on the wild side.

Hates: Things that go bump in the night.

Fact: Rhee is just too cool for ghouls.

Rattle

FYI: Rattle says he's a poltergeist. He thinks poltergeists are posher than ghosts.

Loves: Boo-berry pie and I-scream.

Hates: People who sneak up behind him and shout BOO!

Fact: Rattle's only happy when he's moaning.

Interview with Emma

The Spook Squad's Emma answers readers' questions.

Do you like staying in The Old Tower?

Would **YOU** like staying in a haunted house?

So why do you stay there?

Because I'm not scared of the ghost.

Is anybody scared of Rattle?

Yes, Rattle is – when he sees his own reflection in a mirror!

Which is your favourite Spook Squad adventure?

Bats in the Attic.

Why?

Because I get to fight off a vampire using only a wet lavatory brush!

The Skeleton

Description:
It's all bones and no skin!

Strength:
It doesn't need any-body's help.

Weakness:
It's bone-headed.

Likes:
Trom-bones.

Dislikes:
Body-builders.

Don't say:
'I've got a bone to pick with you.'

Scream Scale Rating:
It's a rattling good monster.

CREATURE FEATURE

The Spectre

Description:
A sight that gives you a fright in the night.

Strength: It can make your nightmares come true.

Weakness: It's not very handy.

Likes: Scaring people.

Dislikes: Bright sunny days.

Favourite food: Ice-scream.

Scream Scale Rating:
It's a scream magnet!

The Werewolf

Description:
It's all paws, claws and jaws!

Strength:
It can smell its prey a mile away.

Weakness:
It's barking mad.

Likes:
Howling at the moon.

Dislikes:
People who call it 'Rover'.

Don't say:
'I bet your bark is worse than your bite.'

Scream Scale Rating:
It gets full marks at full moon!

CREATURE
FEATURE

Chapter One

No Fun at the Fair

The Spook Squad were at the funfair. They wanted to go on all their favourite rides.

'Hey, let's go on the dodgems first,' said Roxy.

'No way,' said Leena. 'I want to go on the Twister – it's evil!'

Nita shook her head. 'Guys, if you want thrills and spills it's got to be the roller coaster.'

'Oh please, can't we just go on the Tea Cup ride?' pleaded Emma.

The other girls looked at her in horror. 'The Tea Cup ride?!' they exclaimed. 'You must be joking, Em.'

Emma wasn't – but before she could say a word, Rattle startled them all by appearing out of thin air.

'You girls had better get over to the Ghost Train fast,' he said. 'Something bad is happening there. I think it may be a job for the Spook Squad.'

'OK! Lead the way, Rattle,' said Leena. But Rattle shook his head, gave a ghostly moan and vanished.

'Huh! Trust Rattle not to stick around if there's trouble,' said Roxy.

'Oh, you are so mean to that poor little poltergeist,' said Emma. 'He's probably just gone to fetch Rhee. She's good at sorting out trouble.'

'She's *too* good at it,' said Leena. 'That's the problem.'

'Yeah, I wish she'd let us deal with the bad guys on our own,' said Roxy. 'After all, we *are* the Spook Squad.'

'So let's get to the Ghost Train pronto, before Rhee arrives and spoils all the fun,' said Nita.

Chapter Two

The Ghost Train

The Spook Squad raced up to the Ghost Train. A crowd of very scared people were demanding their money back from the man selling tickets.

'That ride is way too scary,' said one man. 'It spooked me so much all my hair turned white!'

'But you're bald,' said the ticket seller.

'Yes, but I wasn't when I got on the ride,'

replied the man.

'That's right,' said a woman. 'And this monster jumped in next to me and asked if I wanted to play a game of hide and shriek with it!'

'And did you?' asked the ticket seller.

'Well I shrieked, but there was nowhere to hide,' replied the woman crossly.

'You're pulling my leg,' said the ticket seller.

'No,' said another man. 'But a werewolf was pulling mine. If the train hadn't come out of the tunnel when it did, I wouldn't have had a leg to stand on.'

The ticket seller shook his head. 'Look, there's nothing scary in there apart from a couple of plastic skeletons covered in luminous paint – and they wouldn't even scare my granny!'

'Your granny must be the Wicked Witch of the West then,' said the bald man. 'Cos that ride was like a Halloween party in the Chamber of Horrors – only for real!'

A horrible howling noise came from deep inside the Ghost Train ride.

'Arggghhh!' The crowd all screamed and ran away. Only the Spook Squad and the ticket seller were left.

'What am I going to do?' said the man. 'I'll go bust if everybody's too scared to buy a ticket for the Ghost Train.'

'Don't worry,' said Roxy. 'Give us four tickets and we'll find out what all the fuss is about. We're not scared are we?'

'No way,' said Leena.

'Of course we're not,' said Nita.

'I am – a bit,' said Emma.

But the others were not listening. They had already climbed into the Ghost Train cars.

Emma sighed. All she wanted was to go on the Tea Cup ride and The Ghost Train was definitely not her cup of tea. But she wasn't going to let the others go into danger without her.

'Hey, wait for me,' she yelled.

'Come on then, Em,' yelled Roxy. 'I've got a feeling this ride is going to be *spook*-tacular!'

Emma clambered on board, and with a shake and a shudder the ghost train set off into the dark tunnel.

Chapter Three

Spectres and Skeletons

'Hey, that ticket guy was right.' Leena folded her arms and scowled.

'This ghost train ride is *so* not scary.'

'No, it's rubbish,' said Roxy, slapping away a fake spider that dangled down into her face.

'Yeah,' agreed Nita. 'I mean that old sheet over there isn't going to scare anyone.'

'Well, I'm a bit scared,' said Emma. 'Are you sure it's just an old sheet?'

'Of course I'm sure,' replied Nita.

'Then why has it got eyes that glow in the dark?'

'And fangs,' said Roxy.

'And claws,' said Leena.

'And why is it moving towards us?' asked Emma.

'Err … because I was wrong,' said Nita. 'It's a spectre, not a sheet! Run for it!'

The Spook Squad leapt off the train and dashed off into the shadows. The spectre screamed and came flying after them.

The girls gave the spectre the slip by diving into a giant cauldron. It shot past them and screeched off down the tunnel.

'That was a close call,' said Roxy, as the girls climbed out of the cauldron.

'It was – and we're not out of the woods yet,' said Leena.

'Err … we're in a ghost train ride, not the woods,' said Emma.

'Whatever,' said Nita. 'But we've got company.'

Two grisly skeletons stepped out of a side tunnel and stared at them.

Roxy grabbed Leena's arm. 'Are these guys plastic or real?'

'They're real,' said Leena. 'I can feel it in my bones.'

"But why is that skeleton wearing a kilt?' asked Emma.

'I don't know,' wailed Leena. 'Maybe he's *Boney* Prince Charlie!'

The skeletons rattled towards the Spook Squad.

Leena, Emma and Roxy backed away. But then the sound of barking filled the air. The skeletons stopped. They looked at each other.

'Dog!' they cried. They turned and fled, their bones grinding against each other as they ran.

'Where's the dog?' asked Leena.

Nita stepped out from behind a papier-mâché model of a yeti. 'There isn't a dog. It was me. I figured if you're made of bones the last thing you want to meet is a hungry dog.'

'Hey, you're barking mad, Nita,' said Leena.

'Maybe she is,' said Roxy, 'but it did the trick! Well done, Neet.'

Suddenly the Spook Squad heard loud snuffling and growling noises from deep in the tunnel. Whoever was making the noises was coming nearer and nearer!

'That sounds like a werewolf!' whispered Leena.

'RUN!' yelled Roxy. 'We've got a hell-hound on our trail!!!'

Chapter Four

Emergency Exit

The Spook Squad ducked and dived down the twisting tunnels that made up the ghost train ride. Every time they stopped for breath they heard the sound of paws and claws chasing after them.

'I can't run any more,' gasped Emma. 'I've got a stitch.'

The sound of howling and growling grew louder.

'Hey, that Scream Team of spectres, werewolves and skeletons is closing in on us,' said Nita.

'So what are we going to do?' said Roxy.

Nita gulped and shook her head.

'We can't sort this on our own,' said Emma. 'We need Rhee.'

'We do,' agreed Leena. 'But where is she?'

There was a loud 'POP' and Rattle appeared. 'Rhee's busy dealing with a mummy who's escaped from the museum,' he said. 'But don't panic – I'm here.'

The girls' faces fell.

'Oh great,' groaned Leena. 'Just when we thought things couldn't get any worse.'

Rattle glared at her. 'Oi! Leena, leave the moaning to us ghosts,' he said sharply. 'Now, follow me.'

The Spook Squad raced after the little ghost. He led them to a door marked 'Emergency Exit'. They wrenched it open, jumped out and then slammed the door shut behind them. From inside the ride a hideous yowling started up and claws scratched at the door. The Spook Squad held their breath but, much to their relief, the monsters stayed inside the ride.

'Why aren't they coming out after us?' asked Emma.

'They can't. It's the rules. They have to be invited,' said Rattle.

'Like *that's* going to happen,' snorted Roxy.

'Too right,' agreed Leena. 'But they're still haunting the Ghost Train. We've got to find a way to send them back to Otherworld.'

'Yes, we do,' said Emma. 'Otherwise the poor man who sells the tickets will go bust.'

'Whatever,' said Rattle. 'Anyway, I'm off.

Rhee wants me to meet her mummy.'

The girls groaned, but then Nita's face lit up. 'Hey,' she said. 'I think I know how we can get rid of the Scream Team!'

'How?' asked Roxy.

Nita grinned. 'Trust me. We are going to spook those spooks out of their skins.'

Nita marched the girls over to the Hall of Mirrors. They hurried inside.

Chapter Five

Mirror, Mirror

'Wow!' exclaimed Emma. 'The mirrors in here make you look totally freaky! You can't even recognise yourself.'

Nita grinned. 'Exactly,' she said.

She quickly explained her plan to the others.

The Spook Squad nodded. They took four of the biggest mirrors and carried them out. They set them up in front of the entrance to the Ghost Train ride.

'Right. Now this is where it all gets a bit dangerous,' said Nita. 'Cos now we have to invite the Scream Team to come out here.'

The girls swallowed hard. Then, shaking like jellies in a gale, they climbed back onto the Ghost Train. It sped off into the tunnel.

Two minutes later it came roaring back out with the spectre, the skeletons and the werewolf close behind. The girls leapt off the train and charged over to the mirrors. The Scream Team came racing after them.

Nita, Roxy, Leena and Emma jumped behind the mirrors. The monsters skidded to a halt. They couldn't believe their eyes. The Spook Squad had vanished – and in their place was a bunch of the scariest, nastiest, most hideous fiends the Scream Team had ever seen!

'Yikes!' screeched the spectre. 'Quick, let's go back to Otherworld before these horrors get us!'

They fled back into the Ghost Train ride just as Rhee came running up.

'Are you lot OK?' she said. 'I was dealing with a mummy that should have been a deady – but I've got it all wrapped up now.'

The girls grinned at her. They looked like cats who had just got extra-thick cream with a topping of mouse-flavoured sprinkles.

'Don't worry, Rhee,' they said. 'While you were off playing with your yummy mummy, we've just shown a bunch of monsters that their Scream Team is no match for the Spook Squad's Dream Team!'

It's a Scream!

Spook Squad's Scary Joke Page

Hey Nita, have you heard about the good weather witch?

Yes. She's forecasting sunny spells!

How do witches keep their hair looking good?

They use scare spray!

What do you get if you cross Dracula with Sir Lancelot?

A bite in shining armour!